CYBER SECURITY AWARENESS

*"Amateurs hack systems,
professionals hack people"*

Bruce Schneier

CYBER SECURITY AWARENESS

Employee Handbook

MICHAEL MULLINS

Copyright Notice

Cyber Security Awareness – Employee Handbook

Author: Michael Mullins

Published by: Michael Mullins

Copyright © 2022 Michael Mullins

ISBN: 9798849441375

1st edition (UK English)

Dedication

This book is dedicated to the people who helped me learn everything I know, about electronics, computers, business & life.

Legal Notice

The author of this book has used his best efforts in creating the information contained in it, and neither the author nor publisher make any claim or warranty about the accuracy, completeness or applicability of any information contained in this book.

The author and publisher also disclaim any responsibility for any loss or damages whatsoever, because of reading any information in this book.

All hyperlinks in this book are for information only, and any information available via linked third party websites is not warranted for accuracy or fitness for purpose.

Table of Contents

Foreword

By Brigadier General Jaak Tarien, Retired
and Professor Donna O'Shea

Brig. Gen. Jaak Tarien

Cyber security has long been over-mystified. Today nearly everyone is connected to the internet and thus vulnerable to cyber threats.

Cyber criminals take advantage of careless users by extorting money and valuable data. Nation state backed APT (Advanced Persistent Threat) groups use unaware employees to gain access to business organisations or governmental bodies, to steal sensitive data and advance their political agendas.

Yet far too many users have simply given up on any efforts to defend themselves and their organisations. Cyber security often seems too advanced, too far out of reach and the grasp of the average user.

In Estonia, we have made a deliberate effort to simplify cyber security and educate the public on its basic principles. We have started to call it "cyber hygiene" – just like you have your daily basic routine to take care of your body and surroundings, to minimise risks of catching a virus, you should have a set of hygiene habits for cyberspace.

In his new book "Cyber Security Awareness: Employee Handbook", Michael Mullins has taken an important step towards simplification of cyber security for the average user, both at private and organisational levels. He provides an easy-to-follow guide though the basic threats, and steps that everyone can take to mitigate the risks.

His aim is to create the right mindset for every internet user, providing much needed confidence that basic cyber hygiene, which minimises 90% of threats, is simple and doable for anyone.

Brigadier General Jaak Tarien, Retired
Former director, NATO Cooperative Cyber Defence Centre of Excellence
VP of sales and business development (Defence), Cybernetica AS, Estonia

***

Prof. Donna O'Shea

Cyber security awareness is the process of formally educating a workforce on the various threats that exist, how to recognise them, and the steps to take to keep themselves and their company safe.

This book provides learners with the key knowledge needed for a more cyber resilient workforce, by building awareness on the main cyber security threats they face. It provides a concise explanation on what cyber security is and why it is needed in an organisation.

It identifies the main threats and vulnerabilities facing any organisation, referring to key emerging technologies. It also addresses the challenge of remote working and the essentials of securing a network.

Prevention is highlighted as the primary goal, but the book also provides a guide on what to do if measures have failed, and you fall victim to a cyber-attack.

The material is laid out in an easily accessible style, with chapters including exercises and resources to reinforce learning.

This employee handbook is very suitable for someone who wants the basics on cyber security awareness and what an organisation should consider when building a cyber security awareness programme.

Prof. Donna O'Shea
Chair of Cybersecurity, Munster Technological University, Ireland
Principal Investigator, Confirm SFI Research Centre for Smart Manufacturing
CIT Director Representative, it@cork, Ireland
Board Member, Cyber Ireland

About The Author

Michael Mullins started his career in cyber security after graduating from Middlesex University in London. Prior to that, he worked as an electronics technician.

It wasn't until he caught his first hackers around 1997, that he discovered the power of continuously monitoring computing systems and the users connected to them, as well as reacting quickly to anything out of the ordinary.

Michael was an early adopter of PGP encryption, Linux, and Internet firewalls, and he helped secure organisations of all sizes, including fintech start-ups like Skrill, and multinational luxury brands like Burberry.

He went on to work for several years at IBM, helping them secure their managed services infrastructure at several Swiss banks, and then as Security Officer for one of Switzerland's best known IT companies.

Michael has retained his links to academia and was an external examiner in computer science at a London University. He has written three books, and created courses in cloud computing, Linux, and security. Over 17,000 students have enrolled in his courses online.

In his spare time Michael enjoys mountain biking in the Swiss Alps and running anything from 10 minutes on a treadmill to Olympic distance marathons.

Preface

I experienced teaching for the first time in London, when I taught subjects like control systems and data communications, to undergraduate engineers and computer scientists.

There weren't too many decent computing books in the University library back then, but I was lucky to live near central London, so if I needed to brush up on my knowledge before taking a class, I'd pop down to Foyles or Dillons bookshop, where a geek could easily spend the day reading O'Reilly books, sitting on the floor between the shelves.

Now that we have Amazon, there is so much more choice. What is disappointing though, is that because it's so easy to self-publish an eBook on Amazon, you see books with a great title, but often they are full of waffle and garbage.

So, when I found, myself being asked to teach a course on cyber security awareness to engineers and developers in a Swiss IT company, I thought there must be a good book on this.

I was surprised to find that there wasn't.

But now there is, and you have it in your hands. I hope you enjoy reading it as much as I enjoyed writing it.

Introduction

"Any fool can know; the point is to understand"
Albert Einstein

First, I'd like to thank you for getting a copy of my book on cyber security awareness.

This book has been written with employees in mind, but it is also suitable for students, or anyone who uses computers, smartphones, or any other electronic device, on the Internet. Because nowadays, almost everyone needs a baseline in cyber security awareness.

You probably already know that most employees are given cyber security awareness during their induction day, as well as an annual refresher course to tick a box and satisfy auditors. But surely this is missing the point.

With so many large well-funded organisations becoming victims of ransomware attacks, that cost millions of euros and take months to recover from, isn't it true that the real need for cyber awareness training is to prevent these costly cyber security incidents from happening in the first place.

OK, so what will we be covering in this book?

This book is different to many you will have read before. The layout of the book follows a "what, why, how what if" model of presenting the cyber security concept.

First, we'll clarify what exactly cyber security is. Then we'll look at the reasons why everyone needs training in cyber security. Then we'll highlight how you may be vulnerable to attack by hackers and criminals.

Next, we'll cover the different steps you must take to prevent, cyber-attacks, what to do, and what not to do, if you are ever a victim of a cyber-attack.

There is also a chapter about the UK Cyber Essentials security certification.

You will also find exercises in each section, to help you reinforce your cyber security awareness, as we go through each chapter.

There are also two sections that explain how to report cybercrime that affects an individual, and more serious cybercrime that affects critical services.

At the end of the book there are some useful resources with tools to help you improve your cyber security.

Reading this book and following an accompanying cyber security awareness course, will enable you to better understand the many cyber security threats we all face today, and how to deal with them.

Whatever you learn from this book, your main takeaway should be that better and more frequent training in cyber security awareness, will help reduce the number of costly cyber security incidents, ransomware, and financial scams that we read about in the news every day.

OK, so let's get started.

What Is Cyber Security?

*"Cyber security is the
practice of protecting digital
assets from cyber-attack"*

In this chapter I will present a brief introduction to cyber security. We will look at some basic definitions, a few common cyber-attack types, and their principal causes.

So how do we define cyber security?

"Cyber security is the practice of protecting digital assets from cyber-attack"

You're probably thinking, what exactly are digital assets?

Digital assets include systems, software, and data.

Your personal systems include things like your smartphone, computer, Wi-Fi router, printers, and even smart home devices like security cameras and Amazon Alexa. So, all your electronic devices.

But at work or at school your systems means a lot more.

They include every computer, network, or storage device, that's used in the organisation's information technology (IT).

Because many companies now use public cloud like Amazon's AWS to deliver their IT, some of your systems may be virtual systems in different Amazon datacentres.

Your software includes your PC or MAC operating system, programs installed on your computer, apps installed on your mobile devices, and SaaS apps like Gmail that you use online.

Your data might be private data like your medical records, proprietary data like intellectual property, or public data like web pages.

In a well-managed organisation, data owners must label data to help classify it according to its sensitivity.

Now when we say data, we usually mean all your information that is stored electronically.

But remember that data can also be printed out or written down. So, let's not forget that passwords are data too.

Now an important question you must ask yourself is do you know where all your data is? That's important because you can't protect something if you don't know where it is?

Your data might be on your smartphone, tablet, portable disk drives, on USB sticks, in cloud storage, or even on CD's or DVD's.

So how do we define a cyber-attack?

"A cyber-attack aims to access, change or destroy data, extort money, or interrupt business"

Who is responsible for your cyber security?

In a large organisation everyone is responsible for cyber security. That means company executives, security and IT support teams, and every single person in the organisation. But if you are a solopreneur or a home user, then nobody else is responsible for your cyber security except you.

So, what are the most common types of cyber-attack?

The three most common types of cyber-attack are financial crime, data breaches and ransomware. But sometimes they are combined.

The goal of financial crime is to steal money or crypto assets.

Data breaches are usually carried out to steal valuable private data or proprietary data that can be sold on or used for other crimes.

In the most common ransomware attacks, data is encrypted so that it is no longer usable. Then the attacker demands a ransom payment in return for the decryption key.

So, what are the root causes of cyber-attacks? There are three main reasons why cyber-attacks happen.

Many successful cyber-attacks start with a malicious email. It may be an infected attachment, a link to a malicious website, or a scam to trick someone into disclosing a password or making a payment.

Another reason that cyber-attacks happen is the failure to update or upgrade operating systems and software applications.

And failure to use effective anti-malware software is another big cause of successful cyber-attacks. Even if you fail to update your software, and you open a malicious email attachment, a good anti-malware solution may still save you.

One of the best ways to recover from a cyber-attack is to have regular backups stored off site, for example in cloud storage. And at least some of those backups should be offline or secured against deletion or damage by an attacker.

One final thing you should know is that victims of cyber-attacks are often victims again in the not-too-distant future. Because people are creatures of habit, if you have bad cyber security now, it's unlikely that you will change.

Exercise

Here's a quick exercise for you to do now.

1. First figure out what your most valuable digital assets are.
2. Then consider if they are stored securely.
3. And finally, do you have a secure backup of your data, and where is it?

Why Is Cyber Security Important?

"It takes 20 years to build a reputation, but only 5 minutes and 1 cyber security incident to ruin it"

Now let's look at why cyber security is so important. Well, there are many reasons, but let's look at four big ones. They include compliance, cost, privacy, and national security.

First let's look at compliance.

Often organisations and individuals must demonstrate compliance with customer requirements, laws, or regulations in their region.

For example, if your customer is the British Government, you will be asked for Cyber Essentials Plus security certification.

Or your sales team might ask you for ISO27000 certification, for a sales proposal.

And if you or your organisation processes private data of European Union (EU) citizens, then you need to be compliant with GDPR.

If you process card payments, then you need to be compliant with the Payment Card Industry's Data Security Standard, which is known as PCI-DSS.

And insurers like AXA are now asking if certain security controls are in place, before covering you with cyber insurance.

So, as you can see, there are many reasons why you or your organisation may need to be compliant with cyber security standards.

The bad news is that not being compliant will sooner or later prohibit you from doing business with some customers. But the good news is that by going through the process of achieving and retaining compliance, you will reach an improved level of maturity in your organisation's cyber security.

Now we'll consider the cost of cyber security incidents.

The high cost of cyber security incidents is probably the biggest reason why organisations are beginning to take cyber security more seriously now. Cyber security incidents have many costs, some direct and some indirect. Let's look at a few of them now.

First let's consider direct costs. Direct costs include the cost of recovery, costs to defend legal claims, and fines. Just so you know, IT consultants and lawyers are very expensive, especially in an emergency.

And the cost of preventing a cyber-attack are much less than typical clean-up costs. For example, initial recovery costs for the Irish HSE health service cyber-attack was almost €50 million, but the final figure was estimated to be €100 million.

AMCA in the USA had 20 million people's medical bill data stolen in 2018 and 2019. After $4 million in IT consultant's fees, legal costs, and breach of contract claims, they filed for chapter 11 bankruptcy protection.

The problem is not limited to organisations either. Every year thousands of elderly people are tricked into transferring their savings to scammers pretending to be working for Microsoft support.

But what about indirect costs? Indirect costs include loss of business, damage to reputation and loss of customers.

It's interesting that in the UK, 44% of consumers surveyed said they would stop using a business, after a security breach, and 41% said they would never return. Recently many crypto currency exchanges and start-ups have been hacked, which has done enormous damage to their reputation, and in some cases resulted in bankruptcy.

For example, back in 2014 around 1.5 million Bitcoins, or 7% of the world's supply, was stolen from the Mt. Gox crypto exchange. In 2022 at the time of writing, that was worth around $30 billion. And most of that Bitcoin belonged to ordinary people who could not afford to lose it.

It might seem obvious but often there is an indirect human cost as well. For example, because of the British NHS cyber-attack, many routine medical operations had to be cancelled.

And in 2015, hackers showed that they could remotely control a Jeep's steering and braking systems, over a 4G mobile network.

What About Privacy?

Edward Snowden once said,

> *" Arguing that you don't care about the right to privacy because you have nothing to hide, is no different than saying you don't care about free speech because you have nothing to say"*

Whether you have something to hide or not, your smartphone and computer, harvest a lot more data about you and your behaviours, than you might realise. This data is used to create a profile of you, which is then sold by advertising companies to governments, and anyone else willing to pay for it.

This profile can then be used to target and manipulate you. The goal might be to persuade you to buy something on impulse, or to vote a certain way in the Brexit referendum.

But there is an even darker side. Organised crime networks can also use the same technology and data for identity theft or to exploit you.

So, it's important to ensure that apps and programs on your smartphone and computer are updated and configured for privacy, and that you use modern Internet privacy apps that limit the amount of personal information shared with advertising companies.

Nowadays, with so many past data breaches in companies like Facebook and LinkedIn, you should also think twice about sharing personal information in mobile apps and with social networks.

Next let's look at National Security.

OK, so maybe you don't work for the government. Why should you care about national security? Isn't that someone else's responsibility? Let's try to answer that.

In the past, wars were kinetic, but nowadays electronic wars are being fought in cyberspace.

Cyber warfare can be used to cause anxiety and unrest, by defacing government websites and denying access to essential services like healthcare and banking.

In 2007 after the relocation of a Soviet bronze monument, cyber-attacks targeted several websites of the Estonian government, banks, newspapers, and broadcasters[1] The same kind of cyber-attack just happened in August 2022, but this time the attack was much more powerful.

Since 2007, the Estonian Government has dramatically improved their cyber defences, so the attack had little or no impact this time.

Defacing websites is not a worst-case scenario. Cyber-attacks can also be used to cause physical damage to critical infrastructure.

For example, in 2010, Stuxnet malware was used to damage machinery at an Iranian nuclear facility[2].

Even though the sites industrial control systems were not connected to the Internet, someone carelessly connected an infected USB storage device to the control computer, which enabled the attack. Think about what might happen if a similar attack was used to destroy a nuclear power station near you.

So even if you are just a home user, using cyber security best practices ensures for example that your Wi-Fi router is less likely to be highjacked, to help attack a critical dam or power station.

Exercise

Here's a quick exercise for you to do now.

1. Research one significant data breach in your country and try to find the recovery costs.
2. Based on what we covered in this module, why is cyber security now important to you?
3. Go to the Shodan search engine website at this URL, https://www.shodan.io and see what interesting devices are visible on the Internet.

Threats & Vulnerabilities

"Cyber security is like locking your front door. It doesn't stop burglars, but if it's good enough they will move on to an easier target"

Later we will look at some of the different ways that you may be vulnerable to cyber-attack. But first, it's important to understand how cyber-attacks happen.

For a successful cyber-attack to happen, an attacker (threat actor) must exploit one or more vulnerabilities. And if you are vulnerable, then there is a likelihood that an attacker will exploit your weaknesses.

Some examples of vulnerabilities are, using old software like Windows 7, using open Wi-Fi, and not using good anti-malware software.

The risk level of your vulnerabilities, likelihood of them being exploited, as well as any protection or mitigations you have in place, will affect whether you can be exploited or not.

Think about it. If you leave your front door unlocked at night, you are vulnerable. There is a likelihood that a burglar will exploit your vulnerability, so there is a risk of burglary. And if you lock your door but you have a low quality or badly installed lock, that's a different type of vulnerability.

In the first example (leaving your door unlocked) it is your behaviour that makes you vulnerable, whereas in the second, it's your technology or how you configure it that's the problem. In either example if you add additional protection like installing and setting an intruder alarm at night, your overall risk level is reduced.

Cyber security is no different. if you are careless in your behaviours, you will be a victim of a cyber-attack. And if you use sub-standard technology, or don't use technology properly, the same thing will happen.

Using additional security layers like adding an effective anti-malware solution, will reduce your risk level.

Other options may be to assign the risk to a third party using cyber insurance cover, or you can decide to simply accept some risks.

The following table shows how threats and vulnerabilities can affect the risk of business impact.

Threat	Vulnerability	Risk	Impact
Phishing	No filtering of email attachments or links	Compromise of user credentials	Loss of reputation
	Software not updated	System compromise	Loss of customers
	No awareness training	Spread of ransomware	Legal claims & fines
	No browser protection	Theft of personal data	Cost of recovery
	MFA not used		

Exercise

Here's a quick exercise for you to do now.

4. What are some of your behaviours on social media, that may make you more vulnerable to hackers and scammers?
5. Are there certain websites that you visit or mobile apps that you use from time to time, that may be a risk to your cyber security or privacy?
6. What are the cyber security threats that you are already aware of? Use Google to find others you might not have thought of.

Messaging & Web Browsing

"Never let a computer know you're in a hurry"

We are going to look at vulnerabilities due to using apps for messaging and the world wide web. This includes email apps, instant messaging apps and web browsers.

First, email can expose you to malware delivered in attachments, a malicious hyperlink in a message, or to being manipulated into taking some undesirable action. An undesirable action might be to disclose information, to make a payment, or to start an unwise conversation with the sender.

When reading an email, always look for three things, the sender address, the language & grammar in the email, and the objective of the email.

Hackers often disguise their real email address, so that you think you are receiving an email from someone you know or trust.

By hovering over the sender address you can easily see the sender domain. If it's from the finance director in a large organisation, and the sender domain is @gmail.com, then something is wrong.

If you notice that the language and grammar is bad, there is a good chance that the email is from a scammer.

You already know that email messages are either for your information or meant for you to take an action.

So, when reading any email where there is a call to action like "call me", "reply", "fill in a form" or "click here", ask yourself, what am I being asked to do here, and is that normal.

A sense of urgency is one way to persuade people to take actions without thinking. So, if your managing director emails you asking you to make an unusual payment urgently, then you really should query this with someone else who is senior in the organisation.

If you open an attachment or click on a link in an email, there is a risk that there is malware in the attachment or on the linked website. So, whenever you receive an email that has attachments or links, verify that the sender is genuine, and decide if you should be receiving that attachment or link from that sender, before opening or clicking.

It might surprise you to know that unsubscribe links might also lead to malware.

Some of the most common email threats are phishing, financial scams, and extortion.

Phishing is where you are sent an email to manipulate you into providing confidential information. It could be your password, credit card details or your crypto currency wallet recovery phrase.

Spear phishing is similar, but the difference is a particular person is targeted because of their high value in an organisation. For example, the person who makes payments in a company may be spear phished.

Next, if we look at financial scammers, they may tell you a sad story involving the death of a wealthy person and offer you a share in an inheritance.

And extortion scammers may send you a fake prosecution notice from Interpol or Europol, asking you to pay a fine, or claim to have compromising photos, threatening to release them if you don't pay.

Just like email, you can be sent instant messages to your smartphone, with malicious links, or messages meant to manipulate you into acting. And because instant messaging is mostly used on smartphones, we are mainly concerned with Apple and Android devices.

When we say instant messaging, we are talking about mobile apps like WhatsApp, Facebook Messenger and iMessage, but many other messaging apps as well.

Remember that some mobile devices are more vulnerable to malware, because older Android phones cannot be updated to the latest software version. And many Apple users don't bother to update their phone's software as soon as updates are available. So, they are often vulnerable too.

Even if you receive an SMS or a WhatsApp message with a link from someone you know well, you would do well to ignore the link. This is because family and friends often forward a message to their contacts without realising that it links to malware. And in some cases, a friend's malware infected smartphone will automatically send a malware infected message to all contacts in the phone, including to you.

Often, suspect instant messages will sound too good to be true. The message might say that you have won a big prize, or you might be offered an unusually high discount. Or maybe someone you met only once sends you a message that seems unusual.

If you advertise items for sale on Facebook's Marketplace, you will almost certainly be contacted via Messenger by people who want your items without negotiating the price. The scammer will offer to send a courier to pick up the item and deliver cash for payment. But first you will be asked to pay FedEx transport insurance in advance.

Some people pay the fake FedEx fee, but FedEx never comes with the cash or to pick up the goods.

Another trick to watch out for is crypto influencer scams on Messenger. Someone that you may know as an influencer, sends you a message offering you an exclusive investment opportunity.

Influencers do not send this kind of offer using instant messaging. Usually, the scammers have a cloned Facebook profile, with a much lower number of followers than the real influencer's profile.

Another vulnerability to watch out for is weaknesses in Apple's Airdrop. At a minimum, if your iPhone is set to accept files from anyone, an attacker may send you an embarrassing photo, or even worse, with older versions of IOS, an attacker may be able to install malware on your iPhone.

While we are talking about mobile messaging, it's worth knowing that NIST in the USA, no longer recommends using SMS codes when logging into services like Gmail. Even Google has discontinued SMS login codes for their employees.

This is because of an attack called a SIM swap attack, where someone calls your mobile operator and asks for a replacement SIM. They have then taken over your phone number so that they can receive your SMS login codes.

But SMS messages are also quite easy to intercept using some basic electronics. So, if you are a known high net worth individual, you could easily be targeted this way.

Using a web browser on a computer or mobile device can be equally as dangerous as using email or instant messaging.

One of the biggest issues is visiting websites that spread malware. Let's say for example that you don't want to pay for MS Office. You might search Google for "MS Office Cracked" You will find that the first few sites that Google lists, all contain malware.

So worst case scenario is that you download and install a pirate copy of Office that's infected. Then next time you are on your Internet banking, you might find that your account is almost instantly drained of your savings.

Best case scenario is that your anti-malware solution labels those sites as dangerous, and even if you ignore the alerts and go ahead and click to download, you will be prevented from reaching those sites.

And if you happen to be an aspiring hacker, beware of downloading hacking software like "Dumper Wi-Fi Hacker for PC". This download also contains malware.

A drive-by attack can take advantage of a web browser that contains security flaws due to a lack of security updates. Apart from visiting the infected website, a drive-by doesn't need you to do anything else to launch the attack.

A drive-by attack can be used to spy on you, take over your computer to mine crypto tokens, or to install ransomware.

Another vulnerability in web browsers is the use of browser extensions, and a good example is attacks on hot crypto wallets like MetaMask. Normally when you transfer crypto tokens from your MetaMask wallet, you need to allow the exchange website to spend crypto that's in your browser extension wallet.

The problem is that there have been cases where crypto exchange websites have been hijacked, and quite wealthy users unwittingly allowed the imposter website to spend all their crypto, effectively emptying their wallet of millions in crypto assets.

In extreme cases, malicious browser extensions may also steal a lot of private data, including passwords, or your credit card number.

So, as you can see, there are many ways you are vulnerable to cyber-attack, simply by using email, instant messaging, or a web browser.

Exercise

Here's a quick exercise for you to do now.

1. Check your Junk Email folder and see if you can find example messages that are phishing or financial scams.
2. Check your instant messaging apps to see if you have received messages with a suspicious link.
3. See how secure your browser is by visiting **https://browseraudit.com**

Remote Working

'I'm in a relationship with my neighbour's Wi-Fi. You could say that we have a strong connection'

Next, we are going to look at how mobile workers and people working from home, are also vulnerable to cyber-attacks This became a priority during Covid-19, as IT security teams soon realised that more people working remotely, resulted in increased risk of cyber-attack.

One of the biggest threats to remote workers is because of using public Wi-Fi, or Wi-Fi that's configured with weak security settings.

Why is that?

Ever since the 1990's when Wi-Fi solutions were first standardised, there were major security flaws in the technology, that made it easy to hack into networks. And because Wi-Fi is often configured by people without any cyber security knowledge, sometimes the network is configured with weak security or even with no security.

Because Wi-Fi security standards are extremely complex, it is easy to think that you have configured your network securely, when in fact you haven't.

An example of weak Wi-Fi security is where a restaurant called "Charlies Pizza", uses a Wi-Fi password "CHARLIESPIZZA". And an example of no security is deactivating WEP and WPA encryption, otherwise known as open Wi-Fi.

Another example is where your Wi-Fi is configured to allow connections using a WPS PIN. Nowadays, with the right equipment, an 8-digit PIN can be cracked in about 2 seconds.

To remain anonymous when sharing his stolen data with journalists, Edward Snowden said in his book, that he drove around neighbourhoods until he found Wi-Fi with weak security Once he found a network with weak security, he parked up, hacked it, and then worked on someone else's Wi-Fi.

Once a hacker is connected to your Wi-Fi, in many cases they will be able to connect to your MAC, PC, Apple TV, home camera's, Amazon Alexa, and any other device on your network. And if you have not changed the factory default passwords on your CCTV cameras, then that hacker will also have access to your camera feed.

Hotel Wi-Fi is even more dangerous, since hotel guests are often targeted, and there have been cases in the past where VIP hotel guests like diplomats and company CEO's have been targeted by international hacking groups[3].

There are also vulnerabilities in other wireless devices like keyboards and mice, some using Bluetooth, others that do not. For example, in the MouseJack attack[4], an attacker can hack a computer by sending keyboard commands through a wireless dongle, located up to 100 meters away. And keyboard commands and passwords typed by a user can be sniffed from wireless keyboards in a KeySniffer Attack[5].

In 2019 a security researcher disclosed new vulnerabilities in Logitech USB dongles, wireless keyboards, mice, and presentation clickers[6]. An attacker could use the Logitech dongle to take over a computer without being noticed. So, it's no wonder that Logitech has released a new series of business keyboards, with improved wireless encryption.

And there are plenty of other Bluetooth vulnerabilities that allow an attacker to take over a device using its Bluetooth interface, then stealing or deleting files and so on.

Another less obvious danger to remote workers is IoT (or Internet of Things). People working at home will often have Zigbee compatible smart home controllers. and devices like smart lighting and smart TV's. These are not free of vulnerabilities either. Researchers have found that even smart lightbulbs can be exploited, which can lead to the entire home network being compromised[6].

Another vulnerability that is important especially for remote workers is related to physical access. This is an issue where you may leave your laptop or smartphone unattended, or when they are lost or stolen.

If your laptop does not have disk encryption enabled, then any data on that laptop is at risk if it is stolen, since it is not difficult to get past password protection on many laptops. And having your computer or mobile device encrypted is pointless if you disable screen locks, use a simple PIN code like 0000, or extend screensaver timeouts.

Unencrypted data on USB drives is also exposed if the device is lost or stolen. There are many more serious risks associated with USB devices though, and these are especially relevant to remote workers in public places or hotel rooms.

If you leave your laptop unattended in a public place, it is possible that it can be compromised in a few seconds using a Rubber Ducky Attack[8]. A Rubber Ducky is a $50 custom USB device that acts as a keyboard. It can be programmed to inject enough commands into an unlocked computer, to install malware and take it over in just a few seconds.

There is a $10 alternative that does the same thing. The Bad USB Attack[9] uses a normal USB flash drive that is converted using some custom software, to take over an unattended laptop in the same way.

And in an Evil Maid Attack[10], a laptop's disk encryption password can be captured, by getting access to the unattended laptop, although in this attack, access is needed twice. It's called the Evil Maid Attack because a hotel maid could easily access your laptop in your locked hotel room.

Finally, it's worth mentioning that an innocent looking USB flash drive that you find on the floor, may contain advanced malware that could be used to cause physical damage in a factory, power station or water utility.

So, I hope that by now you can see, how mobile workers and people working from home, are highly vulnerable to cyber-attacks.

Exercise

Here's a quick exercise for you to do now.

1. See if there is an open Wi-Fi network near you. Remember, you don't need a password or passphrase to connect to an open Wi-Fi network.
2. Set a timer for 5 minutes and leave your laptop where you can see it, to test if you need a password to access it again.
3. Check if your computer disk is encrypted by BitLocker (in System & Security on a PC), or FileVault (in Security & Privacy Settings on a MAC).

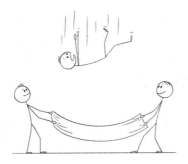

Secure Configuration & Access Management

"Treat your password like your toothbrush. Don't let anybody else use it and get a new one every three months"

Next, we are going to look at how the configuration of your computers, apps and mobile devices affects how vulnerable you are to cyber-attack.

We are going to talk about your anti-malware solution, software updates, how you use a firewall (if you do), and how well you manage your passwords and access.

Let's get started by talking about anti-malware.

Apple computers are not supplied from the factory with an anti-malware application, but Apple's OSX operating system is based on a secure descendent of UNIX, and OSX also has advanced security features, that are extremely effective against malware[11].

But computers that run a recent version of Windows like 10 or 11, have a free built-in Microsoft anti-malware solution. Microsoft's free anti-malware does work well, but it has been shown by some security researchers, to be ineffective against some advanced malware[12].

So, if you are using a free anti-malware product, and neither you nor your IT support have fully configured your Microsoft anti-malware's advanced features, you may be vulnerable.

Effective anti-malware products use advanced techniques like machine learning, to detect threats that have not been detected before. And the best anti-malware solutions will detect installed apps that need security updates.

If you are a home user, and you never visit risky websites, and you access nothing of value on your computer, then you are probably fine with a free anti-malware product like Microsoft's.

But as a business user you must ask yourself, what is the risk level of your organisation, and is your management willing to pay a little more, to avoid being infected by malware or ransomware.

Anti-malware solutions for consumers and for business differ considerably. As well as central management of updates and disinfection, business solutions now provide features like endpoint detection and response (EDR), that automates the detection and reporting of user system intrusions.

Failure to install or properly configure an effective anti-malware solution is one of the top five reasons that users' computers are the source of serious cyber security incidents and ransomware.

Now let's talk a bit about software vulnerabilities.

Every week new software vulnerabilities are discovered in operating systems like Windows, OSX, Linux, IOS and Android, as well as in software apps. From time to time, these vulnerabilities are so severe, that an attacker can get full control over a computer without even being logged in.

So operating systems and software apps on computers and mobile devices must be updated regularly, so that security updates are applied. Companies like Microsoft have an event called "Patch Tuesday" where they release several security updates on the second Tuesday of every month. But updates may be released at any time.

Your home computer will normally be set to install automatic updates, whereas in most organisations, security updates are not applied automatically but through a carefully controlled change management process.

So, if you see a warning that updates are ready to be installed, heed the warning, and install and reboot as soon as you have saved anything you are working on.

You may not be prompted to update apps, or automatic app updates may fail. So, for personal computers it's important to install an anti-malware solution that checks for apps that need updates.

And if all else fails, it's a good idea to check apps like your browser manually to ensure that they are updating by themselves. This is because browsers are closest to the threats you encounter every day on the Internet.

Failure to apply security updates to individual users' computers or computer servers that are used in company infrastructure, is another big cause of cyber security incidents and ransomware.

Another important vulnerability is failure to upgrade old systems with new versions of operating systems and apps when the old ones are no longer supported.

Companies like Microsoft publish various dates on which their products will no longer receive security updates. They refer to these dates as out of support. For example, Windows 7 users will not have received security updates since January 14, 2020, although organisations who pay an update subscription will receive them until January 10, 2023.

These dates are easily found in a Google search or on Wikipedia.

Next let's look at what a firewall is and how it should protect you and others, from cyber-attacks.

For any years, firewalls have been used in cars and in buildings to keep people isolated from potential fires in the engine bay, or in another part of a building. Typically, a firewall is constructed from metal or another fire-resistant material, and there are small openings made for pipes and cables to pass through. A firewall in IT is somewhat similar. It is used to isolate your computer from untrusted networks, and there are a few small openings made for necessary connections.

In cyber security, a firewall is an extra line of defence, that monitors and controls network connections in and out of your computer, or servers in the case of a work or school's IT infrastructure. For example, your firewall may block incoming file sharing connections to your computer but allow your computer to make outbound connections to access printers and the Internet.

Your IT department should be managing the firewalls in your work environment at least for company server infrastructure. But they may not be maintaining a secure firewall configuration on your desktop or notebook computer.

If you are using a modern MAC or PC with Windows 10 or 11, the chances are that your firewall is activated by default.

But just relying on an out of the box default firewall configuration is not very secure, especially at work or at school. Well managed organisations will also use a secure firewall configuration on users' computers, especially if they work at home or remotely via VPN.

Having no firewall or a badly configured firewall on your computer will increase your vulnerability, and the chances of a cyber-attack

spreading laterally within your organisation if your computer or a colleague's is compromised.

Next, we are going to look at how you can be vulnerable if you are not using best practises in managing your passwords and access.

How you use passwords has a big impact on your vulnerability to cyber-attacks. Because many sites like LinkedIn and Facebook are repeatedly hacked, there is a good chance that your passwords for those sites are for sale somewhere on the dark web.

You can check if your passwords have been involved in a data breach using a site like haveibeenpwned.com. If "you have been pwned", and you used your work email address and the same password on a publicly accessible work or school site, then your access those sites is vulnerable.

If you have a weak password, your account can be hacked using a brute force or dictionary attack. These attacks try thousands of possible passwords until the correct password is found.

If your password is cracked or found online, then you are vulnerable, especially if you are not using multi-factor authentication (MFA).

MFA means that you use another factor in addition to your username and password to log in. It could be a code you receive via an SMS, push notification, from an app like Authy or Duo, or from a USB device that you plug into your computer's USB port or phone.

Bad password management and failure to enable MFA, is another big reason why so many organisations end up victims of data breaches and ransomware attacks.

In summary, by being careless with passwords, you are leaving yourself and potentially your colleagues at work or at school, more vulnerable.

By now I think you can see now how an insecure computer configuration and bad access management, can have a big impact on your risk of a cyber-attack.

Exercise

Here's a quick exercise for you to do now.

1. Download the safe example anti-malware test file from the https://eicar.org website. Save it to disk and see if your anti-malware alerts you.
2. See if your account has been compromised in a data breach using the following website https://haveibeenpwned.com
3. Make up a password that you might typically use, but ensure that that you have not used it before, then test it for strength and quality at this site https://password.kaspersky.com

How To Prevent Cyber-Attacks

"Someone has cracked my Gmail password. So now I must rename my cat"

Next, we are going to look at the things you can do to reduce the chances of your cyber vulnerabilities being exploited.

We will cover best practises that you can apply to your everyday use of IT. Many of these measures do not cost you anything, but they will help protect you and your organisation from cyber-attack.

First let's look at using email.

When reading your email, it's important to treat any suspicious email with caution. Three things to look for are sender domain, language in the email and any call to action.

I'm sure you already know what SPAM is, but just in case. SPAM is simply email or other types of electronic messaging, that is sent to you and many others without consent.

Never reply to SPAM. Move it to your junk folder or if you receive multiple messages from the same sender, create a rule to do that for you in future.

Some email apps allow you to report SPAM. If it really is SPAM, do so. But SPAM is not to be confused with email you receive because you joined a mailing list. If you no longer wish to receive email from a list, just unsubscribe from it.

Never open attachments unless you know and trust the person who sent them, and it is normal that they send you attachments.

Avoid clicking on hyperlinks in email messages, even on unsubscribe links, unless you are 100% sure that the sender domain is genuine, and trusted.

Next let's look at Instant Messaging. First, avoid replying to instant messages from people you don't know. But if you must reply, never share personal information on instant messaging apps, for example where you work or where you live.

Beware of fake influencer profiles, and ignore anyone who contacts you with investment opportunities, or offers that are too good to be true.

Just as with email, avoid clicking on any links you receive in an instant message. Assume the link leads to malware, even if the link appears to come from someone you know.

Configure your instant messaging app settings for maximum privacy.

And finally, make sure that your mobile devices' software is updated, and upgraded to the latest OS version. Enable automatic updates where possible.

Next, let's see what you can do to make your web browsing safer.

You web browser is probably one of the apps you use most often in a typical day, but it's also the app that exposes you to more risk.

The most important thing to do is ensure that you are using the latest version of your web browser. For most people this will be automatic, as both Apple and Microsoft include their own browsers in operating system updates.

But automatic updates can fail, so it's worth checking from time to time.

It's also a good idea to configure your browser settings for maximum privacy and security.

When your browser alerts you about an invalid certificate or a malicious site, you should heed the warning and not visit the site.

For an extra line of defence, you should install browser extensions from Malwarebytes, Kaspersky or Microsoft that alert you or block access to malicious sites.

Finally, if you are using an old browser like Internet Explorer, you should use Chrome, Firefox, or Edge instead.

Now let's look at how you can be safe using public and home Wi-Fi.

First, if you manage your own Wi-Fi at home, then try to set your router or access point to use the highest level of Wi-Fi security possible. That might mean only allowing WPA3 for example. Make sure that all your devices still work because some older devices will not support WPA3.

If your router has WPS PIN enabled, you should disable that.

And use a long complex password for your Wi-Fi network. Most Wi-Fi supports passwords up to 63 characters long.

The best way to generate and save a long complex Wi-Fi password is to use the password generator in a good password safe like BitWarden.

And if you want to allow guests to use your home Wi-Fi, then create a separate Wi-Fi network for them to use. This can be done with most Wi-Fi routers and access points.

Always change the default admin password on your home Wi-Fi router and disable remote administration from the Internet.

When using public Wi-Fi hotspots at Starbucks or in hotels, make sure to always connect to your VPN as soon as you connect to the Wi-Fi network. Many VPN clients can be configured to do this automatically.

Home workers responsible for their own IT should also use a VPN if they have any doubts about how to configure Wi-Fi networks securely.

Since open Wi-Fi networks do not require a password to connect, you should avoid using them, because your computer or mobile device is highly vulnerable while you are connected to an open shared network.

If you are on public Wi-Fi and you see warnings in your browser about invalid certificates, you are safer not using that network.

Finally, remote workers should ensure that they are always connected to a VPN, when using Wi-Fi that is not managed by their own IT team.

Next, we will dive into Bluetooth.

Bluetooth devices are vulnerable to many different hacks. The more serious vulnerabilities allow an attacker to install malware on your device, or to capture everything you type from your keyboard, including your passwords.

People working in sensitive jobs in finance, security, military, or government, should avoid using Bluetooth and similar wireless devices, sticking with wired keyboards and mice instead.

If you use IoT enabled devices on your home network, then it is also a good idea to connect them to the Internet via a separate isolated Wi-Fi network.

Next, we will consider physical security and how you can protect your data. You must take extra precautions to prevent data loss if you use a laptop or mobile device in public places.

First, make sure that laptops and other mobile devices have their storage encrypted. Windows 10 Pro uses BitLocker for this, and Apple MAC's use FileVault.

Similarly ensure that any portable storage like USB disks or USB flash drives are encrypted.

If you work in a sensitive role like security or banking, your USB ports on your laptop should be blocked physically or disabled using software.

Never leave your laptop unattended, but if you must, ensure that there is a short screen lock delay, and that you lock the screen before you leave it.

If you manage your own IT, ensure that you have installed a modern advanced antimalware solution like Malwarebytes or Kaspersky.

Software updates and upgrades are also important. Ensure that your computer and mobile devices are configured for automatic system updates, and periodically check that updates are not failing.

Check that apps which can be configured for automatic updates like Microsoft Office and web browsers are in fact updating. Manually update them if necessary.

From time-to-time Microsoft and Apple release major new version of Windows and OSX. In general, you should upgrade your Apple devices immediately, but it is best to wait for at least a year before installing a major new Windows version, for example to upgrade from Windows 10 to Windows 11.

Firewalls can also protect you and prevent malware being spread through networks.

If you manage your own IT, then ensure that at least your Firewall is active on your MAC or PC. If you are an advanced user or want more visibility and control of what network connections are made, then you may want to install a third-party firewall like LittleSnitch on MAC or GlassWire on PC.

Let's look at how to manage access to your services and strong passwords.

Use a trusted password manager like BitWarden that will help you generate and store strong passwords securely. Passwords stored in BitWarden will be synchronised between your various mobile devices and your computer.

Using BitWarden will also help you create a unique password for each service you use, because you never need to remember the passwords stored in BitWarden. But you should use a complex password you can remember as well as a safe multifactor method, to access your other passwords in BitWarden.

Although many browsers like Chrome and Safari support saving passwords in the browser, this is not recommended, because if your computer is compromised, an attacker will have access to your browser and hence all your passwords.

MFA is where you use another piece of information in addition to your password to validate your login. This can be a code you get via SMS, or a mobile app like Authy or Duo, or from a hardware token like YubiKey.

For each web application or mobile app, you use like Gmail or LinkedIn, enable multifactor authentication for login.

So, let's summarise what we have covered.

In this section we have covered many ways in which you reduce your vulnerability and improve your protection against cyber-attacks.

We looked at how to safely use email and messaging, web browsing, Wi-Fi and Bluetooth, physical security and USB devices, anti-malware solutions, software updates, network security with a firewall, password management and multi-factor authentication.

It may seem like we covered a lot. But making improvements to just two or three of those important areas, will make a big difference to your cyber security.

Let's look at one final point that's important to know.

Many cryptocurrency companies proudly boast on their website that they are the most secure crypto exchange or app, only to have millions stolen later, in a very public and embarrassing cyber security incident.

Just know that it is impossible to reach a point where your organisation is 100% secure. Always think of cyber security as a process of continuous improvement.

Exercise

Here's a quick exercise for you to do now.

1. If you don't already have Google Chrome browser, download, and install it.
2. Download and instal the Malwarebytes Browser Guard Chrome extension.
3. Search Google for "Cracked Microsoft Office" and make sure that Malwarebytes warns you if you try to visit the first 2 or 3 sites listed on Google.

What If You Are the Victim of a Cyber-Attack?

"The future depends on what
you do today."

In this section we are going to discuss what you should do if you suspect that you are the victim of a cyber-attack.

To some extent, if you just discovered that your organisation is the victim of a cyber-attack, then it's too late. You have probably lost data, or money or your files have been encrypted and you are being asked to pay a ransom to get them back.

Tough luck, your company is probably going to be on the news and in the newspapers.

That's why the previous chapter about how to avoid cyber-attacks is so important.

Dealing with cyber-attacks such as ransomware in a large organisation is extremely complex and time consuming, and the costs can run into millions. So, this section is only a high-level overview of a generic process that may or may not be followed in your organisation, during a cyber-attack.

The exact cyber incident response process your organisation follows will be determined by your security team and company leadership.

In any case, once you suspect that you may be a victim of a cyber-attack, it's important to follow 7 steps.

1. **Confirm the attack**
2. **Escalate to your IT support**
3. **Contain the attack**
4. **Scope the damage**
5. **Report to authorities**
6. **Inform the public**
7. **Document lessons learned**

If the cyber-attack affects a work or school system, you should only follow steps 1 and 2, unless you work in the security team in your organisation.

If you manage your own personal IT at home, then you probably need to get support from a well-known IT support organisation.

Step #1

Find a way to quickly confirm the attack or decide that it is a false alarm. This may be straightforward if you see your files have been scrambled by ransomware. But there are many other types of attack like denial of service, malware infections, extorsion and data theft. How you confirm the attack will be different in each case.

Step #2

Once you have confirmed a cyber-attack, you must escalate the issue to your IT support or security team without delay. This should be done discretely, since cyber security incidents should not be disclosed to the public, or journalists etc, except by the correct roles in your organisation. Do not try to investigate or resolve the security incidents yourself unless it is your job to do so, and your responsibility.

Step #3

Next, your IT security team needs to contain the damage and limit the spread of malware to other systems. So, if they are dealing with malware or ransomware, they must isolate affected systems, by disconnecting them from the Internet and any other network like Wi-Fi.

Step #4

Then they need to assess and repair the damage. In the case of malware or ransomware, this will mean rebuilding new systems, and restoring data from backups.

Step #5

Depending on where you are, if personal data, medical data, credit card numbers or banking data has been compromised in an attack, your organisation has a legal obligation to report this to the authorities, as well as to the people affected.

Organisations that deliver critical services or digital services in the EU, are also obliged by the Network and Information Security (NIS) directive[13], to report cyber security incidents promptly to the authorities.

Even if your organisation is not obliged to report a cyber-attack to the public, it is better to do so in a controlled communication, as details of the attack may be leaked by an employee anyway.

Step #6

Finally, your IT security team should carry out a root cause analysis and document any lessons learned from the cyber-attack.

That completes this chapter on what to do if you suspect you are the victim of a cyber-attack.

UK Cyber Essentials Certification

"Technology trust is a good thing, but control is a better one."

This chapter looks in detail at the Cyber Essentials Certification program[14], which was developed by the British Government, to help protect the UK population from cyber threats.

Although you may not live in the UK or have any business connections there, the security controls in the standard are very useful to look at, because Cyber Essentials is well suited to organisations whose cyber security strategy is not yet mature, or companies that may not yet have an information security management system in place.

So, what is Cyber Essentials?

The UK Cyber Essentials program is a government backed security certification designed to help organisations of any size improve their cyber security. It was launched in 2014 to help organisations implement a set of simplified security controls that would mitigate the biggest risks with the least effort.

Cyber Essentials was intended to be operated at three different levels, by certification bodies, accreditation bodies and the UK's NCSC (Nation Cyber Security Centre).

There are many certification bodies all around the UK, and these are the organisations that carry out assessments and issue certificates. Since the program started in 2014 there were five accreditation bodies: APMG, CREST, IASME, IRM security and QG. However, since 2020, IASME has been the sole accreditation body. The NCSC oversees the Cyber Essentials program.

In self-assessment, the initial certification that is done online, involves answering a set of questions, in the self-assessment questionnaire (SAQ), and the submission must be signed off by a director of the company. This is not a simple multiple-choice questionnaire. Questions must be answered with freeform input giving details about system configuration.

Cyber Essentials certification is valid for 12 months. For Cyber Essentials self-assessment, organisations are assessed using a questionnaire. For Cyber Essentials Plus, an audit is required at least 3 months after self-certification.

For organisations that wish to have the Cyber Essentials Plus audit, an on-site visit is required. This can be done by one of the many certification bodies.

At the time of writing, the cost of self-assessment was £300 + VAT and this increased to £500 + VAT for bigger organisations.

Cyber Essentials Plus will cost considerably more since the certification body will need to attend site and test the security of systems. If you are in the UK and serious about protecting your organisation from cyber-attacks, then Cyber Essentials Plus is really what you need.

The NCSC's website has all the resources you might need to prepare for self-assessment or Cyber Essentials Plus. Most of the effort will likely be spent on preparing for certification by updating policies and improving security Once you have prepared, submitting the questionnaire will be straightforward.

What Are the Benefits of Cyber Essentials certification?

The biggest benefit of obtaining Cyber Essentials certification is that the going through the process will undoubtedly improve security in your organisation. It also demonstrates commitment to securing supply chains and ensuring that organisations are resilient when faced with ransomware, malware, or other types of cyber-attacks.

Being Cyber Essentials certified also gives an organisation's management a degree of peace of mind, in that they have a good baseline of cyber security in place.

UK domiciled organisations that are certified by an IASME certification body are eligible for free cyber insurance, provided their turnover does not exceed £20 million.

And finally, contracts with central Government where sensitive data is handled or where certain technology is provided will require mandatory Cyber Essentials certification.

What are the Cyber Essentials Security Requirements?

Requirement #1: Firewalls
Boundary firewalls must be used to isolate the organisations digital assets from untrusted networks and devices. Firewalls and network devices must be configured securely. Host based firewalls are recommended for endpoints.

Requirement #2: Secure Configuration
Computers and network devices must be configured securely, by disabling services that are not needed, changing default accounts, and by regularly updating and patching their software.

Requirement #3: User Access Control
This requirement specifies that user accounts should only be available to users who have a valid need for them. In addition, role-based access must ensure that authorised users are only granted access to the digital assets that they specifically have a business need to access. This requirement also covers password policies and multi-factor authentication.

Requirement #4: Malware Protection

This requirement requires that malware is prevented by using either effective anti-malware software, whitelisting of applications or sandboxing. It states that anti-malware signatures must be updated regularly, and protection must include web and file access controls.

Requirement #5: Security Update Management

This final requirement requires that all software on all devices is updated and patched in accordance with best practises for vulnerability management. The requirement also says that software must be licensed and all software that is no longer supported should be removed.

These requirements are sometimes changed, so always check with the official UK Cyber Essentials website for updates.

How Do You Do a Cyber Essentials Assessment?

Step #1: Use the Readiness Toolkit

The UK NCSC has a very useful tool for getting free Cyber Essentials guidance and testing your readiness for the self-assessment. A wizard style questionnaire takes you through some basic questions about your organisation, and your IT infrastructure and devices. You will be given helpful resources and action items to resolve before you are able to be certified.

Step #2: Read the Security Requirements
The NCSC also publishes a comprehensive PDF document with a full set of security requirements that must be met before certification is possible.

Step #3: Make Improvements Needed
Most organisations will need to make some improvements or implement security processes before they can be certified for Cyber Essentials. The questionnaire contains freeform text answers and if the answered are not sufficient certification, will be rejected. This is to be expected because the main objectives of this certification program is to improve security.

Step #4: Choose A Certification Body
To improve your chances of getting certified, look for a more experienced certification body that is also authorised to provide Cyber Essentials Plus assessments. You can also use the tool on the IASME website to select any certification body on the list.

Step #5: Contact Certification Body and Pay Fee
The Cyber Essentials certification bodies will be able to give further advice to assist in completing the SAQ. It's best to contact the certification body directly and discuss the process.

Step #6: Complete the SAQ Online

Once you have received access to the security questionnaire you can complete it in your own time and submit when you are happy that you have answered all questions sufficiently.

So, is Cyber Essentials a waste of money?

Considering that you may qualify for £20 million worth of free Cyber insurance and the average cyber-attack in the UK costs in the region of £3 million, surely, it's a no brainer.

But if you are in the UK, is it necessary to spend all this time and effort getting Cyber Essentials certification?

Well let's see.

In January 2022, the NCSC urged UK organisations to strengthen their cyber security defences, due to tensions between Russia and Ukraine. It was feared that if a military conflict broke out, UK organisations may be targeted with cyber-attacks like those that crippled Estonia for three weeks in 2007.

The NCSC also advised UK organisations to take specific actions to prepare for such an event.

I think it's fair to say they must have had a crystal ball.

Exercise

Here's another exercise for you to do now.

But do <u>not</u> disclose any confidential information about your organisation when answering the questions in this task. Use fictitious answers if necessary.

1. Go to the UK Cyber Essentials Readiness Tool website, and go through the questions to see how you fair https://getreadyforcyberessentials.iasme.c o.uk

Reporting Personal Cybercrime

There is no need to report most personal cyber security incidents. If you have received email with scams or malicious links in instant messaging, then you are not alone. Everyone receives those. And if your computer has been infected by a virus, then you need IT support, not the police.

However, if there is clear evidence that you have lost money to a scammer, you have been threatened, or you are being extorted, then this may be a case where you need to make a criminal complaint to the appropriate police department.

The process is different in every country and state, but the following links will cover at least some of the countries in the EU, Switzerland, and the USA.

European Union

If you live in the European Union and you want to report a significant cybercrime that affects you personally, then you can report it to your local police force. You will find a list of European police forces that handle cybercrime, on the following Europol page.

https://www.europol.europa.eu/report-a-crime/report-cybercrime-online

Switzerland

The Swiss national cyber security centre allows individuals to report cybercrime using a form on the following page.

https://www.report.ncsc.admin.ch/en/chat

For significant cybercrimes you may also approach the federal or cantonal police forces listed on this page.

https://www.bakom.admin.ch/bakom/en/home page/digital-switzerland-and-internet/internet/fight-against-internet-crime.html

United States

Victim of a cybercrime in the United States, can file a complaint with the FBI using their page below.

https://www.ic3.gov/

Reporting Cybercrime Affecting Critical Services

Certain types of incidents must be reported promptly to national authorities in accordance with the European Union's NIS directive and other local legal requirements in your country.

Countries usually have their own national Computer Security Incident Response Teams (CSIRT's). If you need to report significant cyber security incidents that concern essential services or digital services, then you may use one of the national CSIRT's listed on the following URL.

https://anyanylog.com/where-to-report-cyber-incidents/

Summary

Now that we have reached the end of the book, I'd like to thank you for staying with me until the end. Here's a summary of what we have covered.

First, we clarified what exactly cyber security is. Then we looked at the reasons why it's important and why everyone needs training in cyber security.

Then we highlighted how you may be vulnerable to attack by hackers and criminals.

Next, we covered the different steps you must take to prevent cyber-attacks

And we looked at what to do and not do if you are ever the victim of a cyber-attack.

Then we covered the UK Cyber Essentials framework, which is a useful security standard to look at, especially if you don't currently use another cyber security framework in your organisation.

There were two short chapters that explained how to report cybercrime that affects an individual, and more serious cybercrime that affects critical services.

Finally in the following resource section, you will find QR codes that you can scan to get the URL's for some useful tools that can be used to help you evaluate and improve your cyber security.

I hope that you found this book interesting, and that you will use what you learned to improve your cyber security, both at home and in your office.

Resources

The following pages contain the details of different tools that will be useful for testing and improving your cyber security, as well as recovering from security incidents and preventing them happening again.

Virus Test File

The European Institute for Computer Antivirus Research provides a virus test file you can download in different formats.

Anti-malware companies include the EICAR test file in their virus definitions, so it will be detected just the same as a harmful virus.

It is a good tool to verify that your anti-malware software or service is working.

Anti-malware

Kaspersky Labs is a multinational cyber security software company that was founded in 1997.

The company produces different security software and solutions for consumers and for business.

Kaspersky's products have been shown to be the world's most effective against viruses and malware.

Password Checker

Your password is not safe if it can be found using brute force or found in a database of leaked passwords.

This tool allows you to enter a password to test its strength, and to check if it was stolen in a known data theft incident, by checking it in a database of leaked passwords.

The website claims that they do not store passwords you enter to test.

Have I Been Pwned

This site has a database of leaked email addresses, passwords, and phone numbers that you can check.

Although the site appears trustworthy, you should not enter your actual password for any sensitive public website or application, especially if you work in a government, military, or other highly sensitive roles.

Password Manager

Bitwarden is a reliable opensource password manager that is available as a Windows, MAC, iPhone, and Android app. It is also available as a browser extension.

Your login and password data is synchronised across all your devices.

You can also run your own private BitWarden server for your business.

BitWarden offers free and paid plans, and the paid plans offer more security features.

Shodan

This site has a database of devices connected to the Internet that can be reached by anyone.

You can find devices like webcams, printers, industrial control systems and even lightbulbs.

Sometimes people allow connections to their devices on their networks from the entire Internet without realising it.

So, you can use this site to check if you have devices in your organisation that may be more vulnerable because they are reachable from the Internet.

Browser Security Audit

This site allows you to test your browser's security. It's especially useful if you are using an old version of Windows or and old Apple computer that no longer supports browser updates.

But even modern browsers have security issues, so you may be surprised by the results.

Browser Privacy

This browser extension is available for different browsers like Apple's Safari, Google Chrome, and Microsoft Edge.

It provides protection from most third-party trackers while you search and browse the web.

Browser Protection

Malwarebytes Browser Guard detects and blocks unwanted and unsafe content, giving you a safer and faster browsing experience.

It is claimed to be the world's first browser extension that can identify and stop the kind of fake Microsoft tech support scams, that are often used to rob elderly people of their life savings.

Website Malware Test

This site is operated by Forcepoint, which was formally known as Websense.

The site allows you to copy and paste a suspect URL or IP address into the site, to analyse it for malicious content.

This tool is useful if someone sends you a link that you suspect contains malware.

The site does not detect all malware, so use it in conjunction with other website checking tools.

Website Filter Lookup

Usually, larger organisations have web filtering solutions in place to improve security.

Management decides what categories of websites are allowed to be accessed or not.

This site allows you to enter a URL, to see which category it is classified as.

Ransomware Identifier

This website allows you to upload a sample file or ransom demand message if you are the victim of a ransomware attack.

You can usually identify known ransomware you have been infected with and find out if there is a tool available to recover your files without paying a ransom.

References

1. https://www.researchgate.net/publication/357835604_2007_CYBER_ATTACKS_IN_ESTONIA_A_CASE_STUDY
2. https://www.malwarebytes.com/stuxnet
3. https://www.kaspersky.com/resource-center/threats/darkhotel-malware-virus-threat-definition
4. https://www.bastille.net/research/vulnerabilities/mousejack/technical-details
5. https://cyware.com/news/keysniffer-how-an-attacker-can-sniff-your-data-from-250-feet-e42daabd
6. https://www.asiaone.com/digital/logitechs-wireless-dongles-remain-wildly-insecure-and-vulnerable-attacks
7. https://www.bitdefender.com/blog/hotforsecurity/how-your-network-could-be-hacked-through-a-philips-hue-smart-bulb/
8. https://shop.hak5.org/products/usb-rubber-ducky
9. https://www.csoonline.com/article/3647173/badusb-explained-how-rogue-usbs-threaten-your-organization.html
10. https://theinvisiblethings.blogspot.com/2009/10/evil-maid-goes-after-truecrypt.html
11. https://arstechnica.com/gadgets/2022/08/apple-quietly-revamps-malware-scanning-features-in-newer-macos-versions/
12. https://youtu.be/1DG3y3q8_9M
13. https://www.enisa.europa.eu/topics/nis-directive
14. https://www.ncsc.gov.uk/cyberessentials/overview